From Log Cabin to White House with

Abraham Lincoln

BY DEBORAH HEDSTROM

ILLUSTRATIONS BY SERGIO MARTINEZ

FROM LOG CABIN TO WHITE HOUSE WITH ABRAHAM LINCOLN

© 1998 by Multnomah Publishers, Inc.

Illustrations © 1998 by Sergio Martinez

Design by D² DesignWorks

International Standard Book Number: 1-57673-300-9

Printed in the United States of America

For information:
Multnomah Publishers, Inc. - Post Office Box 1720 - Sisters, Oregon 97759

LIBRARY OF CONGRESS CATALOGING-IN-PUBLICATION DATA

Hedstrom, Deborah, 1951-
From log cabin to White House with Abraham Lincoln / by Debbie Hedstrom.
     p.   cm.
    Summary: In a series of letters written between 1856 and 1865, a Washington, D.C.
student describes events in the life of Abraham Lincoln.
    ISBN 1-57673-300-9 (alk. paper)
    1. Lincoln, Abraham, 1809-1865—Juvenile fiction. [1. Lincoln, Abraham, 1809-
1865—Fiction. 2. United States—History—1849-1877—Fiction.
3. Letters—Fiction] I. Title.
PZ7.H3566Fte 1998
[Fic]—dc21   98-16246
                           CIP
                           AC

98 99 00 01 02 03 04 — 10 9 8 7 6 5 4 3 2 1

years ago our fathers

tinent, a new nation, con-

dedication to the proposition

ted equal.

a great civil war, test-

or any nation, so conceived,

ong endure. We are met

MY AMERICAN JOURNEY

Foreword

He floated the Mississippi River, told jokes, wrestled for fun, and rarely made it to a school. But we celebrate his birthday every February, and his face appears on every penny and five-dollar bill. Many of us have even memorized his Gettysburg Address. Remember? "Four score and seven years ago, our fathers brought forth on this continent a new nation...."

Abraham Lincoln was the sixteenth president of the United States, and he was one of the best known and most loved leaders of our country. He took us through the darkest period of our nation's history, when brothers fought brothers and fathers fought sons. The Civil War almost tore our country in two, but President Lincoln helped hold it together.

In this book, *From Log Cabin to White House,* you'll discover how a backwoods boy became president. You'll see him write with a burned stick, hear him split wood, feel the spray of his oars on the river, and laugh at his jokes. You'll also see him cry and pray.

As with all My American Journey books, *From Log Cabin to White House* uses a fictional character to help uncover details of America's history. This time the fictional character is Anne Hampton, a thirteen-year-old girl who lives on East Capitol Street in Washington, D.C. Anne attends Mrs. Howard's Female Academy and visits places that truly existed in 1856, when our story begins. We know they existed because they were mentioned by Frank French, a boy who grew up in Washington, D.C., and kept a diary from 1850 to 1852, starting when he was twelve years old. (If you watch carefully, near the end of the book you may find a clue asking you to imagine how well Frank and Anne knew each other.)

Like this real boy who lived 150 years ago—and probably like you—our fictional character, Anne, goes to school. Sometimes she even gets in trouble there. So like Anne, be prepared to shove aside the butterflies in your stomach and get set to open the door to a new My American Journey adventure!

Introduction

Mrs. Howard's Female Academy - Washington, D.C.
September 1856

Anne walked toward the headmistress's office, taking small steps. The longer it took to get to her doom, the better! *I can't believe I'm getting in trouble,* she thought. *The speaker didn't even look like that silly picture.*

The drawing had gone around the lecture hall while she and the other girls at the academy were waiting to hear a guest speaker discuss "The Progress of Women." They'd all groaned at the thought of listening to another spinster. That's when someone had drawn the picture of a fat lady in a black dress with pulled-back hair who looked remarkably like their last droning lecturer. The picture had circulated as today's speaker—a poised and pretty woman—began her talk. When the picture came to Anne she giggled behind her hands, trying not to be heard. But it must not have worked, because here she was, on her way to the headmistress's office. As soon as the speaker finished her talk, she'd been told to go "at once."

Even though she took small steps, Anne soon reached Mrs. Howard's office. After knocking, she heard a voice call, "Come in!" Taking a deep breath, she squeezed the wire hoop beneath her skirt so she could slip through the doorway—and then stopped in surprise.

With the headmistress was Sarah Josepha Hale, the speaker who had surprised everyone with her high-fashion ruffled silk dress and her soft brown curls. Introduced as the editor of *Godey's Lady's Book,* Mrs. Hale had held all of them spellbound in the lecture hall. She'd spoken of exercise, medical training, and the wearing of fashions that enhanced the female figure instead of dresses that simply followed the latest style. To thirteen-year-old Anne, who liked clothes but struggled with the inactivity of being ladylike, Mrs. Hale's words had been as sweet as strawberries on top of pound cake.

But now, standing in the office, Anne felt panicky. *Surely I won't be reprimanded in front of a guest.*

The headmistress said, "I've called you here because I believe your father and brothers are members of the new Republican Party."

Anne nodded but thought, *Republican Party? What about the silly picture?*

As if in answer to her confusion, Mrs. Hale started explaining. "Besides editing *Godey's Lady's Book*, I am determined to seek the improvement of our country and of women. This means I not only write for the magazine, urging progress, but I also write letters to our political leaders, asking for their support."

The passion behind Mrs. Hale's voice made Anne remember some of the articles she'd read in her mother's copies of *Godey's*. They had spoken of preserving President George Washington's home, building a monument on Bunker Hill, and even making Thanksgiving a national holiday.

Anne shoved these thoughts aside to listen as the editor continued. "To gain support, I must know about the politicians to whom I write," she said. "So this summer I kept track of the Republican convention held in Philadelphia and learned that a new man was gaining national popularity. Have you heard of Abraham Lincoln?"

By now Anne realized she wasn't in trouble. She was even starting to think she might be invited to work for this incredible lady. So she took a moment to think of things she'd heard before answering. "Yes, my father was impressed with the man. After returning from the convention, he said that Mr. Lincoln was honest, a good speaker, and an up-and-comer in the party."

"That is my conclusion also, and I need someone to find out about this man's past, his politics, and his progress," Mrs. Hale said. "That is why I asked your headmistress to recommend a young lady who lived in Washington, D.C., and had Republican relatives and a good pen hand." Looking directly at Anne, she added, "Mrs. Howard suggested you."

Near to bursting with excitement, Anne thought, *I'll be a correspondent just like the one Mrs. Hale hired to report on Queen Victoria in England!* Then another voice inside her head warned, *Not if you act like a giddy child, you won't!*

Immediately Anne folded her hands and tried to appear proper. She looked at Mrs. Hale and said, "I would be delighted to work for you."

After learning more of her duties, getting Mrs. Hale's address, and saying good-bye, Anne rushed to tell her friends the incredible news. This time as she headed down the hall she forgot all about taking small steps. There would be no black dress or tight bun for her—she was going to be a political correspondent for the most popular women's magazine in America!

Chapter One
BAREFOOT BEGINNINGS

Washington, D.C. October 4, 1856

Dear Mrs. Hale,

I take pen in hand to write you because I have learned much about Abraham Lincoln's past. It started when I overheard my brothers telling about Mr. Lincoln splitting logs. Later I mentioned it to my father. That set him to talking!

At first he went on and on about how most young people in 1856 don't know the kind of grit it took to build our country. He told me, "Fifty years ago 'most everybody in this town lived in cabins. Splitting logs was good, honest work, and it still is."

Then Papa went on to tell me how he had cut logs for railroad ties when he was younger than I am now. "Didn't own a pair of shoes until I was ten years old," he said.

"Is that how it was for Mr. Lincoln?" I asked him.

"Pretty near," he said. "His family moved to Indiana when it was little more than a wilderness, and they cleared land along Little Pigeon Creek. Lincoln was swinging an ax from the time he was seven years old."

Listening to my father, I even found out that Mr. Lincoln had plowed fields in his bare feet! Papa said Abe didn't have a pencil, so he wrote some of his lessons with a burned stick. He didn't have paper, either, so he wrote on boards, shaving them off after they got too messy. When he did get some paper, his cousin, Dennis Hanks, helped Abe make blackberry-juice ink. They used a turkey buzzard's quill for a pen!

More than writing, Mr. Lincoln loves to read. Anytime folks get to talking about his past, they mention Abe's book reading. "He'd walk up to fifty miles just to get a new book," they say, and "He used to gather hickory bark for a firelight to read by."

Dennis Hanks, the cousin I mentioned earlier, told others, "Abe used to lay on his stomach by

the fire and read *Arabian Nights* out loud to me and his sister, Sarah. At the end, I told him it was a 'pack of lies.' Abe answered me by saying, 'Mighty fine lies.'"

Even with all this reading and writing, I'm not finding out much about the schools he attended. I know he wrote an essay about not being cruel to animals for one teacher, but I'm pretty sure our up-and-coming politician hasn't had much formal education. His pa moved the family around a lot, and when Abe wasn't working at home, he was hired out to neighbors.

It was his stepmother, Sarah Lincoln, who encouraged Abe's training, even though she can't read or write herself. She married his pa after his mother got a fever and died when Abe was only nine years old. It must have worked out well, having Miss Sarah as his stepmother, because Abe still takes trips to see her to this day.

Losing his mother wasn't the only hard thing in young Abraham Lincoln's life. Twice he almost died himself—once when he was hit in the head by a horse and once when he almost drowned after falling off a log into a creek. In spite of all this, there are lots of good tales about his growing-up years. I guess he was forever pulling pranks or telling stories. One man said, "Abe was always getting up on a stump or a box to make speeches. One day we'd laugh until our bellies hurt, and the next day he'd have us crying with his sad tales."

When I finally saw Mr. Lincoln a few nights ago after a Republican meeting, all I had heard about him made sense. Somehow his poor past and his popularity all blend together to make him seem like a very kind and caring man. He's tall and lean and doesn't give much attention to his clothes. His face looks like it was chiseled out of one of the logs he's split. Yet somehow he seems so real.

It's hard to explain. It's as if Mr. Lincoln doesn't pretend to be something he's not, like some people do. He doesn't put on airs or act all proper and dignified. And when he smiles or gets to talking and joking in his slow, country drawl, others gather around him.

But at my academy and elsewhere around the city, some speak of his poor training and ignorance of national issues. This has made me determined to find more about his life.

I hope this letter finds you in good health and that my information proves valuable to your causes.

Cordially,

Anne Hampton

Chapter Two
FLATBOAT ADVENTURE

Washington, D.C. December 1, 1856

Dear Mrs. Hale,

From wrestling to riverboating, Mr. Lincoln had a lot of adventures after he moved away from his family! I would never have guessed that the tall, sincere man I met after the Republican meeting had lived such a life. But I learned of it from my brothers.

One night while they were playing backgammon, my brothers spoke of what it would be like to float down the Mississippi River on a flatboat. I was trying to read Shakespeare's *Hamlet,* but since it was hard going, I found myself listening to their talk instead. That's when I heard one of them say, "Abe did it."

As it turned out, a flatboat is why Lincoln left home. He'd just built one when two men asked him to row them out to a riverboat. He did so and was amazed when they flipped him two silver half-dollars. My brother quoted Lincoln as saying, "I could scarcely believe that I, a poor boy, had earned a dollar in less than a day by honest work. It made the world seem wider and fairer before me."

Later Lincoln and another of his Hanks cousins took his flatboat down to New Orleans to sell farm produce. Traveling down the Ohio and Mississippi Rivers, they went twelve hundred miles. Once a gang of river thieves attacked them. Fists flying and oars splashing, they escaped.

Another time they watched chained slaves forced onto an auction block to be sold to the highest bidder. Lincoln speaks of it these days when he argues against the Kansas-Nebraska Act and the spreading of slavery into new territories.

This river trip and the discovery that he could earn money eventually led Lincoln to say good-bye to his pa, stepmother, and sister, who had by this time resettled in Illinois. Abe went north and found work in an Illinois river boomtown called

New Salem. He held two jobs, tending a store and logging for a mill.

My oldest brother told me what made Lincoln a town favorite. "Abe's strength in whacking down trees," he said, "led to a public wrestling match with the town champion, Jack Armstrong."

I didn't understand all my brother said about holds, takedowns, and being pinned, but I figured out that Lincoln and Armstrong wrestled to a tie.

"Abe and Jack became fast friends after their bout," my brother continued. "Their match also made the townspeople notice Lincoln."

As I listened to my brothers, I found out some other incredible things. First off, Lincoln's honesty became the talk of the town when he accidentally overcharged a customer by a few pennies and walked miles to return the man's money. Then he asked the local schoolmaster to teach him grammar and proper speech. Soon his tall tales were accompanied by speeches for river improvements. That's when folks started saying, "Abe's a thinker, and he's got a gift for speaking. He should go into politics."

But as it turned out, Abraham went to war instead.

An Indian chief named Black Hawk led his tribe across the Mississippi River, putting the Illinois settlers into a panic. The state militia was called out, and Lincoln joined. Though elected captain, he ended up fighting only mosquitoes, not Indians. Even so he kept his humor.

A friend of mine from the Rittenhouse Boys Academy told me, "Mr. Lincoln served under a colonel who was only four feet, three inches tall. At more than six feet even when slouching, Lincoln dwarfed the man. Still, the colonel corrected Abe for his poor posture. 'Hold your head high, fellow,' he told him.

"Lincoln straightened but not enough for the colonel, who commanded, 'Higher, fellow, higher!'

"Stretching up and extending his neck, Lincoln asked, 'Am I to remain this way always?'

"'Most certainly,' the colonel answered.

"In response, Lincoln got a sad look on his face and said, 'Then good-bye, Colonel, for I shall never see you again.'"

When released from the militia, Lincoln followed the advice of his friends and ran for representative in the Illinois legislature. He lost, but that didn't discourage him. He took jobs as the town postmaster and as deputy surveyor. Then he ran again in the same election two years later and won a seat in the Illinois House of Representatives. One man visiting my father said, "Lincoln was only twenty-four years old when he was elected to public office. But he won because he went among the people. He helped folks with chores, pitched horseshoes, refereed wrestling matches, sat in on quilting bees, and attended dances and wolf hunts."

Elected again two years later, Lincoln made the decision to leave New Salem and move to Springfield, Illinois. I'll learn more of this place and write of it in my next letter.

Thinking about what I've discovered so far, I guess it is true that Mr. Lincoln did not have the best education and training. I've heard many folks say, "It's amazing the man has gotten as far as he has in politics."

With his simple ways and unassuming airs, I do not know if he can go much further.

Most respectfully,
Anne Hampton

Chapter Three
JUDGE AND JOKESTER

Washington, D.C. March 11, 1857

Dear Mrs. Hale,

In an effort to answer your question about how Mr. Lincoln got so popular, I have found every excuse to walk past the Capitol building when Congress ends for the day. I only live a few blocks away on East Capitol Street, but this still isn't an easy task. My mother tends to worry about me because fistfights have broken out between congressmen in and around the Capitol. Our neighbor says it's because of "them gol-darned Southern politicians always causing a ruckus."

But I heard a representative from Georgia say, "Things would simmer down around here if the Northerners would stop trying to tell us what to do."

In spite of the trouble, Mother has agreed a few times to let me walk along Pennsylvania Avenue and listen to the politicians. I think this is because she is proud of my work for you. She even gave me her opinion as to why Abraham Lincoln has gotten so popular. "With all this trouble brewing over slavery, it certainly helped that he married a Southerner, Mary Todd. Though she high-strung, she's taught him more of manners and customs."

For a while I thought my mother's comment would be the only one I'd be able to send to you, because all the talk I heard on the avenue centered on slavery and the fighting it was causing in Kansas. But one day I happened upon a congressman telling another man about Lincoln becoming a lawyer.

He said, "Abe told me he almost became a blacksmith, thinking that was the most suitable work for him. But a friend by the name of John Stuart pushed Lincoln to study law. He helped him learn and even made him his law partner after Abe got his license back in '36. It proved to be a smart move, because Lincoln uses common sense and good stories in court instead of a bunch of fancy legal talk."

Walking behind the men, I also learned that Lincoln became a circuit-riding lawyer, traveling almost five hundred miles on horseback twice a year. I asked a teacher at the academy about circuit-riding lawyers. "A group of lawyers travel with a judge around his assigned circuit twice a year," she told me while circling an area on a state map with her finger. "The judge conducts trials in towns too small to have a full-time court, and the lawyers act as prosecutors and defense attorneys. The travel is primitive. Roads and bridges don't exist in many places, so they wade streams and slosh through mud. Often they must sleep on the floor of farmhouses or double up in tavern beds."

My teacher's explanation helped me understand something else I heard the congressman say. Lincoln entertained his fellow circuit riders most evenings, the congressman said. He'd drape his long legs over the back of a chair and tell stories. One of his favorites was about a slow horse he'd hired one time. "The nag moved like cold molasses, so when I returned it to the stable, I asked the owner if he kept the horse for funerals," Abe would say.

The owner told him no.

"Glad to hear it," Abe would say, "because if

you did, the corpse wouldn't get there in time for the resurrection!"

Thinking back on this story still makes me laugh, but I need to tell you something else the congressman said since I think it explains some of Mr. Lincoln's popularity.

He said, "While Lincoln rode the circuit, he visited people, talking about crops, livestock, children, and politics. He even joined in a wrestling match or two. One lawyer who traveled with him told me that after wrestling a man who challenged him, Lincoln had to go into court with the seat of his pants ripped. The lawyer said when Abe stood up in the front of the room, you couldn't miss the tear. Finally someone sent a note around the courtroom requesting money for a pair of pants for Abe. When the note reached Lincoln, he wrote on the paper, 'I can contribute nothing to the end in view.'"

A few days later I had a chance to tell my father about what I'd heard on the avenue. He laughed at the stories I repeated but added, "Don't be fooled into thinking Abe Lincoln is nothing more than a jokester. Riding the Eighth Circuit, he's gained an excellent reputation for honesty and good sense."

One of Lincoln's law partners, William Herndon, told Papa, "Once he took the case of a Revolutionary War widow who had lost half her

pension to an agent, claiming it for his fee. Before court was over, Lincoln's passion over the injustice done to the elderly woman had half the jury in tears."

Listening to my father, I feel strongly that Abraham Lincoln's honesty must play a big part in his success. But I think his funny stories help, too, and undoubtedly my mother's comment about his wife's influence cannot be overlooked. I hope this answers your question and that you are well. Mrs. Howard's Academy will be attending a congressional session soon, and I should find out more about Lincoln's political life there.

Most sincerely,

Anne Hampton

Chapter Four
A SECOND CHANCE

Washington, D.C. October 21, 1857

Dear Mrs. Hale,

Yesterday my father took me to lunch at the Willard Hotel! It's always bustling with people from the Capitol building and the president's house. President Buchanan even walked in while I was eating some heavenly fried oysters.

Lots of people gathered around him, asking for appointments and favors. I soon feared that the luncheon would not help me discover more of Lincoln. But as my father helped me slip into my cloak, I heard a man say, "When Lincoln was here a few years back, he rivaled Ol' Henry Clay for setting off sparks in the House."

Though it wasn't much of a comment, I didn't know what to make of Lincoln having been in the Capitol before. I asked my father about it as we rode home on the omnibus. "Has Mr. Lincoln ever been elected to Congress?"

"Yes, he has," my father said over the clip-clop of horses' hooves and the rumble of carriage wheels on the cobblestones. "Represented Illinois back in the late '40s. Rented a room in a boardinghouse not far from the Capitol and lived there with his family when Congress was in session. Rubbed shoulders with politicians who went back to the early years of our country—Henry Clay, John Adams, Daniel Webster."

Hearing this, I didn't even look at the ladies' dresses as they strolled down the avenue. Instead I asked, "So why did he leave?"

"Things didn't work out," my father answered. "Abe didn't make much headway in promoting his antislavery sentiments in Congress, even though he sure stirred things up sometimes with his speeches. When then-president Polk declared war on Mexico, Lincoln was against it. He challenged President Polk to show the exact spot where American blood had

been shed first. That's when Abe told Congress, rather sarcastically, 'Young America is very anxious to fight for the liberation of enslaved nations and colonies, provided, always, that they have land.'"

Our omnibus stopped to let people on and off, but I barely noticed. "What happened? What made him return to politics?" I asked.

My father took off his top hat and ran his fingers through his hair—a sure sign that he was thinking. Finally he said, "Lincoln stayed out of politics for almost five years. Heard he went back to Illinois to practice law, and he even took

time to invent a cargo lift for boats.

"But a couple of years ago the Kansas-Nebraska Act started turning those two territories into bloody battlegrounds. Settlers for and against slavery started fighting one another, hoping to get the territory made into a slave or free state. As more and more people on both sides were beaten and killed, Lincoln felt he must take a stand. He ran for Congress again in 1855, saying that slavery should not be allowed to spread and arguing that all new territories should join the Union as free states."

"It's a good thing he was only running in

Illinois," I thought aloud as we got off the omnibus. "No Southerners would have voted for him."

I'm sure I don't have to tell you, Mrs. Hale, slavery has people sizzling. You can't go any place in the capital without hearing of it, especially since the Dred Scott decision said that men of color have no rights. I hear that really upset Mr. Lincoln. While reading at the new Smithsonian Castle, I heard a man say, "Abe Lincoln pointed out that at the signing of the Declaration of Independence, free blacks were full voting citizens in five states. Now a court says they're not. Seems to me our independence is going backward."

The next day I asked my teacher why slavery was dividing the country. She told me slavery was only a side problem. "Money and states' rights are the real issues," she said. "The South needs slaves to work its cotton fields, and it needs low trading fees to ship its cotton overseas. But the North's new factories want high trading fees to keep out foreign products."

"But what of the abolitionists?" I asked.

"They speak up, but they're in the minority," she told me. "Most people don't care about slaves. Look at our city. Twenty percent of our fifty-five thousand citizens are free blacks, Anne, but while you can attend any number of public and private schools, there is only one school for Negro girls your age.

And people of color don't live in homes like yours but in run-down buildings off muddy alleys."

My teacher's words made me think of sections of town that my family avoided. They were known for their shootings, stabbings, and riots. Picturing the dirty, dingy buildings, I wondered how Mr. Lincoln really felt about people of color. A while later, I got my answer in church.

The sermon had been about loving your brother, and after the service a man asked the minister how he could love a black person. "The same way that Abe Lincoln is learning to," the minister answered. "Lincoln started out like most of us, thinking Negroes were lower-class people. But seeing chain gangs, watching slave auctions, and listening to abolitionists is changing him a little every day. Leave your mind open to the truth about all people, and you'll change too."

The fretting and arguing over slavery makes my head spin. Sometimes I don't know what to write to you. But maybe Mr. Lincoln got back into politics and is becoming well known because he has an open mind that keeps learning and growing.

With high regard,
Anne Hampton

Chapter Five

MURDER BY MOONLIGHT

Washington, D.C. December 2, 1858

Dear Mrs. Hale,

I know I haven't written for some time, but having told you all about Mr. Lincoln's past, I needed to wait until he did something of note. He has! News of the murder trial and the debates he's involved in have made it to Washington quickly, even though Lincoln is still in Illinois.

I learned of the murder while attending the play *Uncle Tom's Cabin* at Ford's Theater. At intermission, I lingered in the hall, admiring the side boxes with their satin-and-lace curtains and fancy chandeliers. That's when I overheard two ladies talking. "At the trial, tears ran down Mr. Lincoln's cheeks," the taller one said, "when he spoke of the young man's widowed mother losing her only son to a hangman's noose. My sister, who lives in Springfield and heard it, said it was most heart-wrenching."

"I have little doubt of that," the shorter woman replied, "but my John says it was a brilliant stroke on Lincoln's part to use the almanac in defending the son. The eyewitness admitted he was 150 feet away from the fight but said the night's moonlight allowed him to clearly see the widow's son strike and kill the victim. By using the almanac, Lincoln proved that on the night of the murder the moon had already set when the murder occurred—so there wasn't nearly enough light to see from so far a distance."

I listened for the trial's outcome, but instead the women started talking about the actor playing Uncle Tom. So I left to search the lobby for my father. Finding him, I asked about the murder trial.

"Lincoln got the young man off," he told me. "From all I heard, he put on a splendid defense. And it wasn't the only case he's won. Just recently he defended the Illinois Central Railroad and got himself a five-thousand-dollar fee." Lowering his voice, he added, "Talk in the party is that Lincoln can now pay for a strong congressional campaign."

My father's words came true when the Republicans in Illinois nominated Lincoln to run against Stephen Douglas for U.S. senator. Abe's speech accepting the nomination caused a real to-do. In it he said the country was "a house divided." He told the convention, "I believe this government cannot endure, permanently, half slave and half free. It will become all one thing, or all the other."

In addition, Mr. Lincoln challenged Mr. Douglas to seven debates. Everywhere people speak of them; thousands of listeners gather to hear the two candidates in every city that hosts a debate. I even heard the Lincoln-Douglas debates mentioned at the circus a few days ago. My friends and I were clapping for a man who walked on glass bottles when a boy near us said to his pals, "Did you hear what Abe Lincoln said at the last debate? It was first rate!"

His friends shook their heads, and I listened with them as the boy told what happened. "After going on a bit, Douglas called Lincoln two-faced. Later, when it was Abe's turn to speak, he mentioned the insult and said, 'I leave it to my audience. If I had another face, do you think I would wear this one?'"

The debates are also in the newspapers regularly. I picked up one that said Douglas spoke with a commanding voice and impressive gestures while Lincoln had a gawky figure and made absurd up-and-down movements for emphasis. In spite of this, the journalist ended by writing, "Yet the open-minded person felt at once that, while on one side a skillful debater argued for a wrong and weak cause, there was on the other side a thoroughly earnest and truthful man defending sound convictions."

Though Lincoln spoke well and ran a good campaign, he lost the election. I found out more of this when my academy went to visit the Capitol building. We were to see the House of Representatives, but a boys academy was already there, so we went into the Senate. This proved fortunate, because there I heard two senators talking about the election.

"After losing, Lincoln said he felt like a boy who had stubbed his toe—too big to cry and too badly hurt to laugh," one of the men said.

"Maybe so," the other senator replied, "but he'll be on the rise now, probably in a national election next time."

At first I thought I heard the man wrong. *How could losing an election help Mr. Lincoln?* I wondered.

Leaning forward in my seat, I listened carefully as the man continued, "Douglas is a top politician, yet he only won by carrying the state senate districts. More people actually voted for Lincoln, but Douglas's party won more seats in the Illinois sen-

ate, and it's the state senates that select the U.S. senators. Believe me, the Republicans will take notice of this raw backwoodsman. They'd be fools not to."

The rest of the time in the Senate was boring until a fight broke out between a Southern congressman and a Northern senator. Mrs. Howard rushed us out, and we went back to the academy. One of my friends, who is a bit of a tomboy, grumbled as we walked. "I bet the boys academy didn't have to leave."

As she grumbled, I looked at the "stump." It's the half-finished pillar started a long time ago to honor George Washington. Then I looked back at the half-finished top of the Capitol building and its two unfinished additions. With all the North and South problems, I wonder if these huge projects will ever be finished.

The torn-up buildings. The Senate fight. They made me think of Mr. Lincoln's speech about a nation divided not being able to endure. If he ever does get elected to a big office, I sure hope he can do something to fix things.

Respectfully,
Anne Hampton

Chapter Six

HALF HORSE, HALF ALLIGATOR

Washington, D.C. November 18, 1860

Dear Mrs. Hale,

Part of Washington is cheering, and part is in a pucker. Mr. Lincoln's getting elected as president has people split down the middle. Northern newspapers are printing "Let the People Rejoice!" while Southern papers say, "Evil Days Are Upon Us!" I even heard one of my brothers say that Lincoln is getting hate mail every day.

A few months ago, I might not have believed my brother, but now I think it's true. Living in the capital, I've heard Mr. Lincoln called plenty of names, but mostly the jokesters poked fun at his tall awkwardness or his humble background. Like the man who called him "half horse and half alligator." Most of those things were just said in fun. But these days I hear him called terrible names I can't even repeat. Then at church a week ago, a member told my father, "My brother in Florida wrote that folks are hanging man-sized dolls by the neck with 'Lincoln' signs pinned to them."

But the worst thing happened when I went to get President Buchanan's autograph. He will be leaving when Mr. Lincoln takes over the presidency in two months, so Mrs. Howard said that now was our last chance to get the fifteenth president's signature.

I got the autograph, but when I was walking down the front hall of the president's house, two men burst in the door. "They're leaving the Union," one was saying, "and talking of forming the Southern confederacy."

"South Carolina's representatives have always been hotheaded," the second man replied. "It's probably just one more threat. But we'd best tell Buchanan, though I doubt he'll do much."

I didn't walk home but hurried to an omnibus. I kept wanting to tell the driver to go faster. I had to tell my father what I'd heard. He would know what to do. But he didn't. He just shook his head and

said, "It was bound to come. Tensions have been running too high for too long."

"But Father," I interrupted, "what will become of our country? Surely you can do something!"

"No, Anne," my father said as he laid a comforting hand on my shoulder. "We cannot control the actions of others, only our own. And as for our country, I fear a civil war. I do not envy Abraham Lincoln his new presidency nor the decisions he must make."

I went up to my room and plopped on my bed, unmindful of my hoop skirt. Sitting there, I thought back to all the excitement in our home when Mr. Lincoln gave his first big lecture and then when he got the presidential nomination and won the election.

My brothers went all the way to New York City to hear Mr. Lincoln's speech. In spite of the large crowd that attended, my older brother said, "At first I believed all was lost. On stage Lincoln looked tall and awkward. His clothes were wrinkled and didn't fit well. When he said 'Mr. *Cheerman*' instead of 'Mr. *Chairman*,' I thought, *This won't do. This might work in the country, but it will never go down in New York City!*

"But when Lincoln got warmed up, his gestures smoothed out, his face lit up with his passion, and he was transformed. I forgot his rumpled clothes,

gangly height, and unruly hair. Soon I was on my feet with everyone else, yelling like a wild Indian.

"Walking out of the hall, I saw a fellow all aquiver like myself and asked him what he thought of Lincoln the rail-splitter. He said, 'He's the greatest man since Saint Paul.'"

A few months later both my father and brothers went to the Republican convention that nominated Lincoln for president. They returned with glowing reports. "It was close. Real close. But when the winning vote was taken, thousands of us cheered wildly," my father said.

During the campaign, I proudly wore a Lincoln button on my cloak, and one of his coins dangled from my bracelet. My father and brothers spoke often on Lincoln's behalf, and our whole family could hardly sleep the night the votes were counted.

Thinking about it now, I can't understand how the thrill of learning Abraham Lincoln won the presidency could change so much. Right now I just feel afraid of war. Lying down on my bed, I confess, I had a good cry.

Sadly yours,
Anne Hampton

Chapter Seven

YANKEE AGAINST REBEL

Washington, D.C. July 2, 1862

Dear Mrs. Hale,

President Lincoln looks different these days—more chiseled and graver even when he laughs and smiles. He's taken to wearing a beard too. I've heard people say the change is due to mistakes made early in his presidency that caused lost battles. Others think it is the death of yet another of his sons. I don't know who is right, but at a neighbor's barbecue I heard Lincoln tell his friend, Mr. Seward, "I enjoyed politics immensely before becoming president. I was even eager to hold the highest office in the land. But in the president's house, instead of glory, I've found only ashes and blood."

It's not just the president's house that seems so grim. Soldiers and tales of battle fill our city. When Southern troops marched against us, Union regiments rushed to defend the capital . . . and they just kept coming. Now tents and uniforms fill all our open spaces: the Capitol grounds, the Georgetown College campus, and lots of other areas.

Thousands of wounded soldiers crowd our hospitals too. I volunteer in the one closest to my home. A clerk from the patent office, Clara Barton, is organizing the volunteers and doing a good job in maintaining supplies. Also a poet named Walt Whitman helps to tend the wounded. But even with these fine people to work beside me, sometimes I just want to go home. I am not sure if it is the work or the heartache of torn bodies and death.

Both my brothers joined the fighting, and sometimes what I see at the hospital makes me feel a cold fear for them. I pray each night that God will somehow keep them safe against cannon, rifle, and saber.

I write many letters for the wounded soldiers in the hospital, who are often terribly homesick. Like myself, they've never been far from home before. Since pen and ink are scarce, usually I can only

write their letters in pencil. But I think they'd use burned sticks and boards if it were the only way to send news home. In fact, one day at the post I saw so many letters I mentioned it to the clerk. She told me, "The war is causing folks to write like never before. Most days we handle ninety thousand letters, and the bigger post office—the one in Louisville—handles twice that many."

While the soldiers write letters, the president is becoming known for writing pardons. My father says it has riled some of the officers, and General Butler even sent Lincoln a telegram saying, "I pray you not to interfere with the courts-martial of the army. You will destroy all discipline among our soldiers."

"The very next day," my father told me, "an old man came to the president, asking for a pardon for his son. He read Butler's telegram to the old man and said he could do nothing. The man looked so sad that Abe reached for paper and wrote, 'Job Smith is not to be shot until further orders from me —A. Lincoln.'

"Still unhappy, the elder Smith said, 'But you could order him shot tomorrow.'

"Lincoln smiled at that and said, 'If your son never dies until orders come from me to shoot him, he will live to be a great deal older than Methuselah.'"

The president's humor and storytelling during these dark days anger some folks. One day while I waited to see the president about getting more quinine and brandy for the hospital, I heard a congressman yelling at Lincoln. The walls did not stop his harsh words. "That is the way with you, sir— story! story! You are the father of every military blunder that has been made during this war. You are on the road to perdition, sir."

How I wished I could have prevented the man's words! I know the president feels the weight of every battle lost and every person slain. His stand on the war and ending slavery has been attacked on every side: by abolitionists, conservatives, states' righters, and armchair generals. But how can anyone lay this war at only his feet? Besides, he told my father why he jokes. "I laugh in these dark days of war," the president said, "because I must not cry."

I do not believe that laughter always stops our president's tears, and he, too, is in my prayers along with my brothers. I believe he thinks the only thing that can justify the terrible loss of life in this war is permanent freedom for the slaves.

Faithfully,
Anne Hampton

Chapter Eight

THANKSGIVING

Washington, D.C. December 19, 1863

Dear Mrs. Hale,

 Listening to my father thank the dear Lord for our many blessings on the last Thursday of last month, I felt a new hope stir within me. Mrs. Hale, you were right. During this dark time, we need to somehow be thankful. I'm glad you've kept on for all these years, writing hundreds of letters and many editorials in an effort to establish a national day of thanksgiving.

 Your letter requesting the holiday must have seemed a breath of fresh air to the president after the battle at Gettysburg. Many say the South will never recover from the blow of its losses. So many men died! My own younger brother was wounded there and is now home. To this day he does not speak to me of the fighting.

 It took time for news of his injury to reach us, but when it did, my father left to bring him home. After returning, Father said, "Gettysburg is not a place for the fainthearted. Even now, four months after the battle, piles of coffins still wait for burial."

 He also said that while waiting for my brother's release, he heard the president speak at the dedication of the national cemetery being established there. "The main speaker went on for more than two hours," my father told us, "yet I cannot remember what he said. The president followed with a speech of only ten sentences, yet I will never forget a single word."

 As his speech at Gettysburg showed, the war has deeply affected President Lincoln. He doesn't laugh as much these days, and when I saw him last, I could tell he has lost weight. Many say he does not sleep well. Yet every day he presses on. He even visited the hospital where I volunteer. Walking among the rows of beds, he stopped in amazement when he saw a soldier taller than himself whose feet hung off the cot. Grinning, he held out his hand to the fellow and said, "Hello,

comrade, do you know when your feet get cold?"

Both men shared a fine laugh, and it was good to know that the war hadn't taken away all the president's humor.

A much shorter soldier also caught the president's attention recently. Johnny Clem is only twelve years old, but a Confederate cavalry captured him in October. Immediately officials made plans for his exchange. He is a kind of national hero since newspapers printed his story about a year ago.

Johnny tried to join the Union army when he was only nine years old. Turned down, he tagged along with a Massachusetts regiment until the men made Johnny their drummer boy. He went on to survive the battles of Chickamauga and Shiloh, earning the nickname "Johnny Shiloh." Last I heard, he is to be made a general's aide, and he has changed his name to John Lincoln Clem.

For those of us working to relieve the suffering of the soldiers, there is yet another reason for gratitude. The U.S. Sanitary Commission believed it had to disband due to lack of money, but volunteers in Chicago thought of having a "Sanitary Fair" to raise funds. Five thousand people paid to tour the exhibits, eat, and attend an auction. People bought pianos, toys, clothes, flowers, and other donated items. The item that brought the most money came

from President Lincoln. He donated the original draft of the Emancipation Proclamation, and it sold for three thousand dollars!

Since then our town and many others have held similar fairs. It's almost a competition to see who can put on the best auction and earn the most money. Our city did well, but both New York and Philadelphia raised a million dollars!

Walking home from the hospital, I see even more reasons to give thanks. The Capitol building is finished! Its new iron dome is tall and stately, and its added wings make it look like a palace. Now only the Washington Monument remains unfinished.

I think that someday there will also be a Lincoln Memorial. The president has done so much, including issuing the Proclamation of Amnesty and Reconstruction. It promises full pardons to all who resume allegiance to the United States.

Though this awful war is not over, my father says this offer of pardon provides a way for our country to mend and heal when the fighting finally stops.

Yes, I had much to be thankful for on America's first national Thanksgiving—especially for the Almighty giving our country a man like President Abraham Lincoln to take us through our darkest hour.

With thanks,

Anne Hampton

Epilogue

DARKNESS AND LIGHT

Washington, D.C. December 10, 1865

Dear Mrs. Hale,

Your need for information about the president is long past, and your campaign for a national Thanksgiving holiday is a success. But I wanted to write and congratulate you on the publishing of your recent book, *Sketches of Distinguished Women*.

As I read it, I could almost see you as you were years ago, speaking to my class at Mrs. Howard's Academy. Though you have long had a passion for your causes and for women's rights, you have always looked, spoken, or acted like a fine lady. I can think of no better person to write about distinguished women.

I was also happy to see that some of President Lincoln's jokes were published in a book. These days his humor and easy ways tend to get lost in the memories of his terrible death. How well I recall my own horror and tears upon learning that the president was shot while attending a play in Ford's Theater.

It seemed so senseless. The Civil War was over, and full pardons had been promised to all.

If only that awful John Booth could have realized that murdering the president would make it worse for the South, not better! Instead of President Lincoln's easy pardons, the Southerners have ended up with a program of punishment—plantations and arms have been seized, and carpetbaggers have made it rich off the South's misery. Even today, I sometimes think, *If only the president had lived.*

I do not believe I will ever forget Mr. Lincoln's last speech. It took place two days after Lee had surrendered, ending the war. Three thousand people cheered in our streets. Then Lincoln stood at a window in the president's house and spoke to the crowd about putting the country back together. From my position, I heard a man yell, "What shall we do with the Rebels?"

From among the crowd, another yelled, "Hang them!"

That's when I saw Lincoln's son, Tad, get his father's attention and speak to him. Straightening up after stooping to hear his son, Mr. Lincoln said, "That's right, Tad. We don't want to hang them. We want to hang on to them."

Shortly after that speech, I attended the president's funeral. Our entire city mourned. The hospital volunteer and poet, Walt Whitman, even wrote a poem called "O Captain! My Captain!" that echoed our sorrow.

I did not watch the entire procession accompanying the black-draped carriage. Too many tears had given me a terrible headache. Later, when I felt better, my father came and spoke to me. His words gave me comfort.

He said, "Right before Gettysburg, I went to the president's house to speak with Mr. Lincoln. He seemed more confident than he had for a long time, and I asked him why.

"He told me, 'Yesterday, I felt that we'd reached a great crisis. I went to my room, knelt down, and prayed. Never before had I prayed with so much earnestness. I felt I must put all my trust in almighty God. He gave our people the best country ever given to man. He alone could save it from destruction. I had tried my best to do my duty . . . and found myself unequal to the task. The burden was more than I could bear. I asked him to help us and give us victory. When I got up, I was sure my prayer was answered.'"

Remembering my father's words now, years later, I realize that God did answer President Lincoln's prayer. Neither Mr. Booth nor the vengeance-driven politicians stopped God's answer, for once again, we are the United States of America.

Sincerely,

Anne Hampton French

here on a great battle field
come
[struck] to dedicate a portion

for
ing place of those who

that nation might live

are proper that we po

But in a larger sen

we can not consecrate——